Rachel Carson

By Justine and Ron Fontes

Consultant
Linda Bullock
Curriculum Specialist

C
A Division
New York Toronto London Auckland Sydney
Mexico City New Delhi Hong Kong
Danbury, Connecticut

Designer: Herman Adler Design
Photo Researcher: Caroline Anderson
The photo on the cover shows Rachel Carson.

Library of Congress Cataloging-in-Publication Data

Fontes, Justine.
  Rachel Carson / by Justine & Ron Fontes.
    p. cm. — (Rookie biographies)
  Includes index.
  ISBN 0-516-25896-6 (lib. bdg.)   0-516-26819-8 (pbk.)
  1. Carson, Rachel, 1907-1964—Juvenile literature. 2. Biologists—United
States—Biography—Juvenile literature. 3. Environmentalists—United States—
Biography—Juvenile literature. I. Fontes, Ron. II. Title. III. Rookie biography.
  QH31.C33F66 2005
  570'.92—dc22

                    2004015314

9 10 R 14 13   62

Do you love plants, animals, and the ocean?

This girl is holding a starfish.

This is Rachel Carson.

Rachel Carson did!

She wrote about plants and animals and how to take care of them.

Carson was born on May 27, 1907. She grew up on a farm in Pennsylvania.

Carson spent a lot of time with her little dog and her Mom.

This is Carson with her dog, Candy.

Carson looked at baby birds like these.

Carson's mother loved nature.
She taught Carson to look
closely at plants and animals.

So, Carson explored the woods
and creeks near her home.
Then she would ask questions
about what she saw.

Carson also learned from books and magazines. Her favorite magazine had stories that children wrote.

When Carson was ten, she wrote a story about a brave pilot. The magazine printed her story and gave Carson a prize!

ST. NICHOLAS

FOR · BOYS · AND · GIRLS

SEPTEMBER · 1918

Carson's story was printed in this magazine.

Carson is dressed in her graduation cap and gown.

Carson kept writing stories and winning prizes. Everyone was sure she would become a writer.

In college, Carson decided to study nature instead. She studied hard and got good grades.

Many scientists work at Woods Hole Marine Biological Laboratory.

Carson studied nature at the
Woods Hole Marine Biological
Laboratory in Massachusetts.

There, she saw the ocean for
the first time.

Carson used a typewriter to write stories.

Carson got a job writing radio shows about fish. She also wrote for magazines and newspapers.

Carson wrote every night after work. She wrote so well that she was asked to write a book.

Carson's first book was called *Under the Sea Wind*. She wrote about the many plants and animals that live in the ocean.

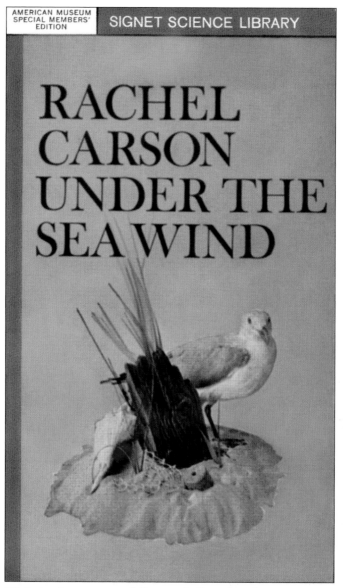

SIGNET SCIENCE LIBRARY

RACHEL
CARSON
UNDER THE
SEA WIND

This is the cover of Carson's first book.

Scientists wore diving suits, like these, to explore the ocean.

Carson went underwater in a diving suit. She wanted to know what it was like to be a fish!

Carson also sailed on a research ship. She was the only woman scientist on the ship.

Carson wrote a second book. It was called *The Sea Around Us*.

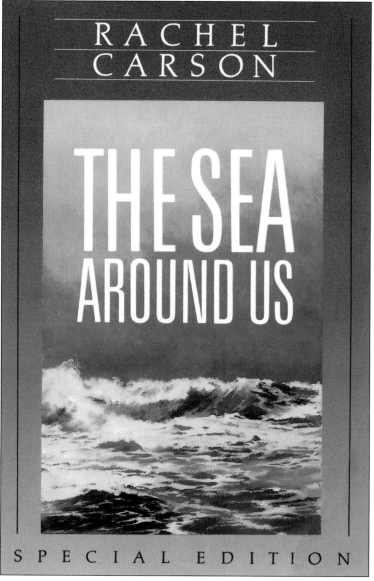

RACHEL
CARSON

THE SEA
AROUND US

SPECIAL EDITION

This is the cover of Carson's second book.

One day, Carson got a letter from her friend Olga. Olga had found dead birds in her yard. These birds were killed by bug poison.

Carson decided to study the poisons used to kill the bugs.

This farmer is spraying bug poison.

Carson found out that the poisons used to kill bugs killed other things, too.

She wrote a book called *Silent Spring*. The book was a warning about using poison.

Carson used a microscope to learn about many things.

John F. Kennedy was the 35th president of the United States.

Even the President listened to Carson!

Soon there were laws to help keep the Earth and living things healthy. Carson helped make the world a better place.

Laws help protect birds and trees like these.

Words You Know

diving suits

magazine cover

poison

President John F. Kennedy

Rachel Carson

Index

About the Author

Justine and Ron Fontes have written over 350 children's books. They have written all kinds of books, both fiction and nonfiction. They are avid readers and supporters of nature. They live in Maine with three adorable cats.

Photo Credits

Photographs © 2005: AP/Wide World Photos: 28, 31 top; Beinecke Rare Book and Manuscript Library, Yale Collection of American Literature: 7, 12, 16; Corbis Images: 25, 30 bottom (William Gottlieb), 29 (Lynda Richardson); Dembinsky Photo Assoc./Sharon Cummings: 8; Magnum Photos/Erich Hartmann: cover, 4, 31 bottom; Used by permission of Oxford University Press, Inc.: 23 (book jacket from *The Sea Around Us*, by Rachel Carson, copyright 1950, 1951, 1961 by Rachel Carson, renewed by Roger Christie); Penguin Group USA: 19 (cover of *Under the Sea Wind*, by Rachel Carson, c 1941 Signet Science Library); PhotoEdit/Myrleen Ferguson Cate: 3; Rachel Carson Council, Inc./Brooks Studio: 27; St. Nicholas Magazine, For Boys and Girls, September, 1918, c 1918 by the Century Co.: 11, 30 top right; Superstock, Inc./ Underwood Photo Archives: 20, 30 top left; Time Life Pictures/Getty Images/ Fritz Goro: 14.